J. E Sweetser

Pilgrim Melodies

J. E Sweetser

Pilgrim Melodies

ISBN/EAN: 9783337038601

Printed in Europe, USA, Canada, Australia, Japan

Cover: Foto ©Lupo / pixelio.de

More available books at **www.hansebooks.com**

PILGRIM MELODIES.

A COLLECTION

OF TUNES ADAPTED TO HYMNS IN THE

"Songs for the Sanctuary,"

AND OTHER

PROMINENT COLLECTIONS

FOR CHURCH WORSHIP.

BY

J. E. SWEETSER.

A. S. BARNES AND COMPANY,

NEW YORK, CHICAGO AND NEW ORLEANS.

PREFACE.

THE contents of this volume were originally composed and arranged for the use of the Choir of the CHURCH OF THE PILGRIMS, (REV. DR. STORRS) in Brooklyn, by Mr. J. E. SWEETSER, who was Organist and Director for several years previous to his death. The tunes were never intended for publication, but the earnest solicitations of friends for copies of the various pieces made it necessary to put them in some available shape.

They are printed just as originally written, and as endeared to the hearts of those who heard them sung Sabbath after Sabbath.

The entire collection is copyright property and will be defended accordingly.

FRED. W. LOVEJOY.

INDEX OF TUNES.

NOTE.—The numbers refer to Hymns and Pages in SONGS FOR THE SANCTUARY Edition with Tunes.

Metrical Index of Tunes.

DIMAN.

J. E. S.

1. How vain is all beneath the skies! How transient ev - ery earth - ly bliss! How slen - der all the fond - est ties, That bind us to a world like this!

2 The evening cloud, the morning dew,
    The withering grass, the fading flower,
  Of earthly hopes are emblems true—
    The glory of a passing hour!

3 But though earth's fairest blossoms die,
    And all beneath the skies is vain,

There is a land, whose confines lie
  Beyond the reach of care and pain.

4 Then let the hope of joys to come
    Dispel our cares, and chase our fears:
  If God be ours, we're traveling home,
    Though passing through a vale of tears.

BERGEN.

HYMN 377. L.M. Arr.

1. The morn - ing kin - dles all the sky, The heavens re - sound with an - thems high, The shin - ing an - gels as they speed, Proclaim, "The Lord is risen in - deed!"

2 Vainly with rocks his tomb was barred,
   While Roman guards kept watch and ward;
Majestic from the spoiléd tomb,
   In pomp of triumph, he has come!

3 When the amazed disciples heard,
   Their hearts with speechless joy were stirr'd;
Their Lord's belovéd face to see,
   Eager they haste to Galilee.

4 His piercéd hands to them he shows,
   His face with love's own radiance glows;
They with the angels' message speed,
   And shout, "The Lord is risen indeed!"

5 O Christ, thou King compassionate!
   Our hearts possess, on thee we wait;
Help us to render praises due,
   To thee the endless ages through!

BEAUTIFUL ZION.

HYMN 1298. L. M. 6l.   J. E. S.

1. Beautiful Zi-on, built a-bove, Beau-ti-ful cit-y, that I love, Beauti-ful
gates of pearl - y white, Beauti-ful temple,—God its light! He who was slain on
Cal-va-ry Opens those pearly gates to me, Opens those pearly gates to me.

2 Beautiful heaven, where all is light,
Beautiful angels, clothed in white,
Beautiful strains that never tire,
Beautiful harps through all the choir!
There shall I join the chorus sweet,
Worshiping at the Saviour's feet.

3 Beautiful crowns on every brow,
Beautiful palms the conquerors show,
Beautiful robes the ransomed wear,
Beautiful all who enter there!
Thither I press with eager feet;
There shall my rest be long and sweet.

4 Beautiful throne for Christ our King,
Beautiful songs the angels sing,
Beautiful rest, all wanderings cease,
Beautiful home of perfect peace!
There shall my eyes the Saviour see: ·
Haste to this heavenly home with me!

HOPE.

J. E. S.

1. Would you see Je - sus? come with prayer,
And heart re - pent - ant, to his feet; None who will
right - ly seek him there, Shall fail his face of
love to greet, Shall fail his face of love to greet.

2 Would you see Jesus? come with faith,
 And search the word his grace hath given,
For help and guidance in the path
 That leads to his abode in heaven.
Would you see Jesus? day by day
 Let thought and converse be on high,
And hastening on the heavenward way,
 With Jesus live, with Jesus die.

SHINAR.

HYMN 1296. L. M.   Arr.

1. As when the wea - ry trav - eler gains The height of

some o'er - look - ing hill, His heart re - vives, if

'cross the plains, He eyes his home tho' dis - tant still:—

2 So when the Christian pilgrim views,
By faith, his mansion in the skies,
The sight his fainting strength renews,
And wings his speed to reach the prize.

3 'Tis there, he says, I am to dwell,
With Jesus in the realms of day!
Then I shall bid my cares farewell,
And he will wipe my tears away!

O, THOU THAT HEAREST.

HYMN 623. L. M. D.

SOP. SOLO.

1. O, thou that hear'st when sin - ners cry, Though all my crimes before thee lie,

Be - hold me not with an - gry look, But blot their mem-'ry from thy book.

2. Cre - ate my na - ture pure with-in, And form my soul a - verse to sin;

Let thy good Spir-it ne'er de-part, Nor hide thy presence from my heart.

3 I cannot live without thy light,
Cast out and banished from thy sight;
Thy holy joys, my God, restore,
And guard me, that I fall no more.

4 Though I have grieved thy Spirit, Lord,
His help and comfort still afford;
And let a sinner seek thy throne,
To plead the merits of thy Son.

PALMER.

HYMN 557. L. M.   J. E. S.

1. Trembling before thine awful throne, O Lord! in dust my sins I own:

Jus-tice and mer-cy for my life Contend! oh, smile and heal the strife!

The Sav - iour smiles! up - on my soul   New tides of
The Sav - iour smiles!   up - on my soul New tides of

New

hope   tu - multuous roll;   His voice proclaims my par -don

hope   tu - multuous roll;   His voice pro - claims   my par-don
hope   tu - multuous roll;   His voice, his voice proclaims my par-don

tides of hope tu - multuous roll;   His voice pro-claims   my par-don found Se - raph-ic transport wings the sound. Earth has a joy unknown in heaven,

The new-born peace of sin for-given ! Tears of such pure and deep de - light,

Ye an-gels ! never dimmed your sight. Ye saw of old, on cha - os rise

The beauteous pil - lars of the skies ; Ye know where morn, ex- ult - ing springs,

And evening folds her drooping wings. Bright heralds of th' e - ter - nal Will,

A-broad his er - rands ye ful - fill; Or, throned in floods of beamy day,

Symphonious, in his presence play. But I a - mid your choirs shall shine,

And all your knowledge will be mine: Ye, on your harps must lean to hear

A se - cret chord, A se - cret chord that mine will bear.

GOD OF MY LIFE!

HYMN 635. L. M.

1. God of my life! thro' all   my days   My grateful pow'rs shall

sound thy   praise;   The song shall wake with op' - ning   light,

And war - ble to   the   si - lent night.   When anxious care would

break my   rest,   And grief would tear my   throbbing breast,

Thy tune-ful prais-es rais'd on high, Shall check the mur-mur and the sigh. When death o'er na-ture shall pre-vail, And all my pow'rs of language fail, Joy thro' my swim-ming eyes shall break, And mean the thanks I can-not speak.

But, oh! when that last con-flict's o'er, And I am chained to flesh no more, With what glad accents shall I rise To join the mu-sic of the

Soon shall I learn Which ech - o

skies! Soon shall I learn th'ex-alt-ed strains Which ech-o

Which ech - o

o'er the heavenly plains, And em - u - late, with joy un-known,
And em - u - late,

The glowing seraphs round thy throne, The glowing seraphs round thy throne.

HYMN 377. L. M.

Quar. (The morning kin - dles all the sky, The heavens resound with anthems high,
Solo. 2. (Vainly with rocks his tomb was barred, While Roman guards kept watch and ward;
Solo. 4. His piercéd hands to them he shows, His face with love's own radiance glows;

The shining an - gels as they speed, Proclaim, "The Lord is risen in - deed!")
Ma - jes - tic from the spoiléd tomb, In pomp of triumph, he has come!)
They with the an - gels' message speed, And shout, "The Lord is risen in - deed!"

3. When the amazed disciples heard, Their hearts with speechless joy were stirred;
5. O Christ, thou King com - pas - sion - ate! Our hearts possess, on thee we wait;

Their Lord's be - lov - ed face to see, Ea - ger they haste to Ga - li - lee.
Help us to ren - der praises due, To thee the endless a - ges through!

LYCIA.

HYMN 264. L. M. D.

Arr.

1. The spacious fir-ma-ment on high, With all the blue e-the-real sky,

And spangled heavens, a shining frame, Their great O-rig-i-nal proclaim;

Th' unwearied sun, from day to day, Does his Cre-a-tor's power dis-play;

And publish-es to ev-ery land The work of an al-might-y hand.

2 Soon as the evening's shades prevail,
The moon takes up the wondrous tale;
And nightly, to the listening earth,
Repeats the story of her birth;
While all the stars that round her burn,
And all the planets in their turn,
Confirm the tidings as they roll,
And spread the truth from pole to pole.

3 What though in solemn silence, all
Move round the dark terrestrial ball,—
What though no real voice nor sound
Amid their radiant orbs be found,—
In reason's ear they all rejoice,
And utter forth a glorious voice,
Forever singing as they shine,—
"The hand that made us is divine."

CONFIDENCE.

HYMN 788. L. M. D.

J. E. S.

1. Though sorrows rise and dangers roll, In waves of darkness o'er my soul;
2. Though Sinai's curse, in thunder dread, Peals o'er mine unpro-tect - ed head,
3. Oh,   by the pangs thyself hast borne, The ruffian's blow, the tyrant's scorn,

Though friends are false and love de - cays, And few and e - vil are my days;
And   memory points, with bus - y pain, To grace and mer-cy given in vain;
By   Sinai's curse, whose dreadful doom Was bu - ried in thy guiltless tomb;

Though conscience, fiercest of my foes, Swells with remembered guilt my woes;
Till   na - ture, shrinking in the strife, Would fly to hell to 'scape from life;
By   these my pangs, whose healing smart Thy grace hath planted in my heart—

Yet   ev'n in na-ture's ut-most ill, I   love thee, Lord! I love thee still!
Though every thought has power to kill, I   love thee, Lord! I love thee still!
I   know, I feel thy bounteous will, Thou lov'st me, Lord! thou lov'st me still!

HYMN 1240. L. M. 7 lines.

J. E. S.

1. E - ter - ni - ty! e - ter - ni - ty! How long art thou, e -
ter - ni - ty! And yet to thee time hastes away, Like as the war-horse
to the fray, Or swift as couriers homeward go, Or ships to port, or
shaft from bow; Pon - der, O man, e - ter - ni - ty, e - ter - ni - ty!

2 Eternity! eternity!
  How long art thou, eternity!
  As long as God is God, so long
  Endure the pains of hell and wrong,
  So long the joys of heaven remain;
  Oh, lasting joy! oh, lasting pain!
  Ponder, O man, eternity!

3 Eternity! eternity!
  How long art thou, eternity!
  O man, full oft thy thoughts should dwell
  Upon the pains of sin and hell,
  And on the glories of the pure,
  That do beyond all time endure;
  Ponder, O man, eternity!

CHILDREN OF GOD.

HYMN 686. C. M.

1. Children of God, who, faint and slow, Your pil - grim path pur - sue,
3. Oh! weak to know a Saviour's pow'r, To feel a Fa - ther's care;

In strength and weakness, joy and woe, To God's high call - ing true!—
A moment's toil, a passing show'r, Is all the grief ye share.

2. Why more ye thus, with linger-ing tread, A doubting mournful band?
4. The orb of light, though clouds a-while May hide his noon-tide ray,

Why faintly hangs the drooping head? Why fails the fee - ble hand?
Shall soon in lov - lier beau - ty smile To gild the clos-ing day,—

5. And, bursting thro' the dusk - y shroud That dared his power in - vest,

Ride throned in light o'er ev - ery cloud, Triumph - ant to his rest.

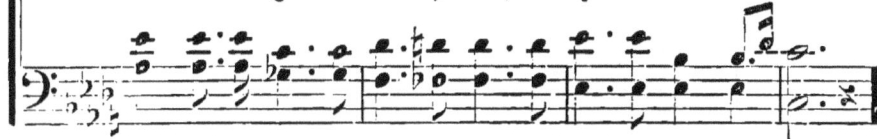

6. Then, Christian, dry the fall - ing tear, The faithless doubt re - move;

Redeemed at last from guilt and fear, Oh! wake thy heart to love.

NATICK.

1. When I can trust my all with God, In tri-al's fear-ful hour,—

Bow all re-signed beneath his rod, And bless his spar-ing power;

A joy springs up a-mid dis-tress, A fountain in the wil-der-ness.

2 Oh! to be brought to Jesus' feet,
  Though trials fix me there,
Is still a privilege most sweet;
  For he will hear my prayer;
Though sighs and tears its language be,
The Lord is nigh to answer me.

3 Then, blessed be the hand that gave,
  Still blessed when it takes;
Blessed be he who smites to save,
  Who heals the heart he breaks:
Perfect and true are all his ways,
Whom heaven adores and death obeys.

HYMN 1234. C. M.

J. E. S.

1. There is an hour when I must part With all I hold most dear; And life, with its best hopes, will then As noth-ing-ness ap-pear. 2. There is an hour when I must sink Beneath the stroke of death; And yield to him who gave it first, And yield to him who gave it first, My struggling vital breath.

3 There is an hour when I must stand
  Before the judgment-seat,
And all my sins, and all my foes
  In awful vision meet.

4 There is an hour when I must look,
  On one eternity;

And nameless woe, or blissful life,
  My endless portion be.

5 O Saviour, then, in all my need
  Be near, be near to me:
And let my soul, by steadfast faith,
  Find life and heaven in thee.

22 SAMARIA.

HYMN 833. C. M.

1. Our blest Re-deem-er, ere he breathed His ten-der, last fare-well,

A Guide, a Com-fort-er bequeathed, With us on earth to dwell.

He came in tongues of liv-ing flame, To teach, convince, sub-due;

All-powerful as the wind he came, And all as view-less, too.

2 He came, sweet influence to impart,
A gracious, willing Guest,
While he can find one humble heart
Wherein to fix his rest.
And his that gentle voice we hear,
Soft as the breath of even,
That checks each fault, calms every fear,
And whispers us of heaven.

3 And every virtue we possess,
And every virtue won,
And every thought of holiness
Is his and his alone.
Spirit of purity and grace!
Our weakness pitying see;
Oh, make our hearts thy dwelling-place,
Purer and worthier thee!

HYMN 553. C. M.

Arr.

1. O thou, from whom all goodness flows, I lift my soul to thee;

In all my sor-rows, con-flicts, woes, O Lord, re-mem-ber me!

When on my ach-ing, burdened heart My sins lie heav-i-ly,

Thy par-don grant, new peace im-part· Thus, Lord, re-mem-ber me!

2 When trials sore obstruct my way,
  And ills I cannot flee,
Oh, let my strength be as my day—
  Dear Lord, remember me!
When in the solemn hour of death
  I wait thy just decree;
Be this the prayer of my last breath:
  Now, Lord, remember me!

FATHER! HOW WIDE THY GLORY SHINES!

HYMN 249. C. M.

1. Fa - ther! how wide thy glo - ry shines! How high thy wonders rise!

Known thro' the earth by thousand signs, By thou - sand thro' the skies.

Those might - y orbs pro - claim thy pow'r, Their mo - tions speak thy skill;

And, on the wings of ev' - ry hour, We read thy pa - tience still.

But, when we view thy strange design To save re - bel - lious worms,

Where vengeance and com - pas - sion join In their di - vin - est forms,—

Here the whole De - i - ty is known; Nor dares a crea - ture guess,

Which of the glo - ries brightest shone, The justice, or the grace.

Now the full glo - ries of the Lamb A - dorn the heav'nly plains;

Bright se - raphs learn Im - man - uel's name, And try their choicest strains.

And try their choicest strains, And try their choicest strains.

And try their choicest strains, And try their choicest strains.

Bright se - raphs learn Im - man-uel's name, And

Bright se - - raphs learn Im - - man - uel's name, Bright

Bright se - raphs learn Im - man - uel's name, Bright

Bright se - - raphs learn Im - - man - uel's name, Bright

try their choic - - est, their choic - est strains.

se - raphs learn Im - man - uel's name, And try their choicest strains.

Bright se - raphs learn Im - man - uel's name, And try their

choic - est, their choic - est strains. Oh! may I bear some

hum - ble part, In that im - mor - tal song; Won - der and

joy shall tune my heart, And love com - mand my tongue.

WITH SONGS AND HONORS SOUNDING LOUD.

HYMN 255. C. M.

With songs and hon - ors sounding loud, Address the Lord on high;

O - ver the heav'ns he spreads his cloud, And wa-ters vail the sky.

He sends his show'rs of blessings down, To cheer the plains be - low;

He makes the grass the mountains crown, And corn in valleys grow.

His stead - y coun - sels change the face Of the de - clin - ing year;

He bids the sun cut short his race, And win - try days ap - pear.

UNISON.

His hoar - y frost, his flee - cy snow, De - scend and clothe the ground;

The liq - uid streams forbear to flow, In i - cy fet - ters bound.

TRIO.

He sends his word and melts the snow, The fields no long-er mourn;

He calls the warm-er gales to blow, And bids the spring re-turn.

The changing wind, the fly-ing cloud, O-bey his mighty word:

With songs and hon'-ors sounding loud, Praise ye the sov'reign Lord.

HYMN 566. C. M.

Arr.

1. Be mer-ci - ful to me, O God! Be mer-ci - ful to me;

For tho' I sink be - neath thy rod, Yet do I trust in thee.

2 Thou art my refuge, and I know
    My burden thou dost bear,
And I would seek, where'er I go,
    To cast on thee my care.

3 Thou knowest, Lord, my flesh how frail,
    Strong though my spirit be;
Oh, then assist, when foes assail,
    The soul that clings to thee.

4 And, gracious Lord, whate'er befal'
    A thankful heart be mine,—
A heart that answers to thy call,
    One that is wholly thine.

5 And may I ne'er forget that thou
    Wilt soon return again,
And those who love thy coming now,
    Shall shine in glory then.

BARTON.

Arr.

1. I heard the voice of Je - sus say,—"Come un - to me and rest; Lay down, thou wea - ry one, lay down Thy head up - on my breast!" I came to Je - sus as I was, Wea - ry, and worn, and sad,

I found in him a rest-ing-place, And he hath made me glad.

I found in him a rest-ing-place, And he hath made me glad.

2 I heard the voice of Jesus say,—
  "Behold, I freely give
The living water; thirsty one,
  Stoop down, and drink, and live!"
I came to Jesus, and I drank
  Of that life-giving stream;
My thirst was quenched, my soul revived,
  And now I live in him.

3 I heard the voice of Jesus say,—
  "I am this dark world's light;
Look unto me, thy morn shall rise
  And all thy day be bright!"
I looked to Jesus, and I found
  In him my Star, my Sun;
And in that light of life I'll walk,
  Till all my journey's done.

MALTA.

Arr.

1. Thou art my hid-ing place, O Lord! In thee I put my trust;

En-cour-aged by thy ho-ly word, A fee-ble child of dust:

I have no ar-gu-ment be-side, I urge no oth-er plea;

And 'tis e-nough my Sav-iour died, My Sav-iour died for me!

2 When storms of fierce temptation beat,
  And furious foes assail,
My refuge is the mercy-seat,
  My hope within the vail:
From strife of tongues, and bitter words,
  My spirit flies to thee;
Joy to my heart the thought affords,
  My Saviour died for me!

3 And when thine awful voice commands
  This body to decay,
And life, in its last lingering sands,
  Is ebbing fast away;—
Then, though it be in accents weak,
  My voice shall call on thee,
And ask for strength in death to speak,
  "My Saviour died for me."

HYMN 1303. S. M.

1. Come, sing to me of heav'n, When I'm a-bout to die·
Sing songs of ho-ly ec-sta-sy, To waft my soul on high.
There'll be no sor-row there, There'll be no sor-row there,
In heav'n a-bove, where all is love, There'll be no sor-row there!

2 When the last moment comes,
　Oh, watch my dying face,
To catch the bright seraphic glow,
Which on each feature plays.
　　There'll be no, &c.

3 Then to my raptured ear
　Let one sweet song be given;
Let music charm me last on earth,
And greet me first in heaven!
　　There'll be no, &c.

MY SHEPHERD WILL SUPPLY MY NEED.

HYMN 928. C. M. D.

1. My Shep-herd will sup-ply my need, Je-ho-vah is his name; In pas-tures fresh he makes me feed, Be-side the liv-ing stream.

He brings my wand'-ring spir-it back, When I for-sake his ways; And leads me, for his mer-cy's sake, In paths of truth and grace.

3.

When I walk through the shades of death,
  Thy presence is my stay;
A word of thy supporting breath
  Drives all my fears away.
Thy hand, in sight of all my foes,
  Doth still my table spread;
My cup with blessings overflows,
  Thine oil anoints my head.

3.

The sure provisions of my God
  Attend me all my days;
Oh, may thy house be mine abode
  And all my works be praise:
There would I find a settled rest,
  While others go and come,—
No more a stranger, or a guest
  But like a child at home.

MANVILLE.

HYMN 261. S. M.

J. E. S.

1. Oh! bless the Lord, my soul! His grace to thee pro - claim;
2. Oh! bless the Lord, my soul! His mer - cies bear in mind;

And all that is with - in me join To bless his ho - ly name.
For - get not all his ben - e - fits: The Lord to thee is kind.

SOPRANO SOLO.

3. He will not al - ways chide; He will with pa - tience wait; His

wrath is ev - er slow to rise, And read - y to a - bate.

ALTO SOLO.

4. He pardons all thy sins, Prolongs thy fee-ble breath; He heal-eth thy in -

firm-i - ties, And ransoms thee from death, He healeth thy in - firm-i - ties,

And ransoms thee from death. 5. Then bless his holy name, Whose grace hath made thee

whole; Whose loving-kindness crowns thy days; Oh! bless the Lord, my soul!

LODI.

HYMN 684. S. M. D.

1. Soldiers of Christ, arise, And gird your armor on, Strong in the strength which God supplies, Through his e-ter - nal Son: Strong in the Lord of hosts And in his mighty power, Who in the strength of Jesus trusts, Is more than conqueror.

2 Stand, then, in his great might,
  With all his strength endued,
And take, to arm you for the fight,
  The pamoply of God:
That, having all things done,
  And all your conflicts past,
You may o'ercome through Christ alone,
  And stand complete at last.

3 From strength to strength go on;
  Wrestle, and fight, and pray;
Tread all the powers of darkness down,
  And win the well-fought day.
Still let the Spirit cry,
  In all his soldiers, "Come,"
Till Christ the Lord descends from high,
  And takes the conquerors home.

MELTON.

HYMN 786.   7s. 6 lines.

Arr.

1. Shepherd, with thy tenderest love Guide me to thy fold a-bove;

Let me hear thy gen-tle voice; More and more in thee re-joice;

From thy full-ness grace re-ceive, Ev-er in thy Spir-it live.

2 Filled by thee my cup o'erflows,
For thy love no limit knows:
Guardian angels, ever nigh,
Lead and draw my soul on high;
Constant to my latest end,
Thou my footsteps wilt attend.

3 Jesus, with thy presence blest
Death is life, and labor rest;
Guide me while I draw my breath,
Guard me through the gate of death,
And at last, oh, let me stand,
With the sheep at thy right hand.

BALLARD.

J. E. S.

1. An - gels! roll the rock a - way; Death! yield up thy

might - y prey; See! the Sav - iour leaves the tomb,

Glow - ing with im - mor - tal bloom. 2. Hark! the won - dering

an - gels raise Loud - er notes of joy - ful praise;

Let the earth's re - mo - test bound

Ech - o with the bliss - ful sound.

3 Saints on earth, lift up your eyes,—
Now to glory see him rise
In long triumph through the sky,
Up to waiting worlds on high.

4 Heaven unfolds its portals wide!
Mighty Conqueror! through them ride;
King of glory! mount thy throne!
Boundless empire is thine own.

5 Powers of heaven, seraphic choirs,
Sing, and sweep your golden lyres;
Sons of men, in humbler strain,
Sing your mighty Saviour's reign.

6 Every note with wonder swell,
Sin o'erthrown, and captive held!
Where, O death, is now thy sting?
Where thy terrors, vanquished king?

PARAN.

HYMN 1006. 7s. D.

J. E. S.

1. When our heads are bowed with woe; When our bit-ter tears o'er-flow;

When we mourn the lost, the dear, Je-sus, Son of Ma-ry, hear!

Thou our fee-ble flesh hast worn; Thou our mor-tal griefs hast borne;

Thou hast shed the hu-man tear: Je-sus, Son of Ma-ry, hear!

2 When the heart is sad within,
With the thought of all its sin;
When the spirit shrinks with fear,
Jesus, Son of Mary, hear!
Thou the shame, the grief, hast known;
Though the sins were not thine own,
Thou hast deigned their load to bear:
Jesus, Son of Mary, hear!

3 When our eyes grow dim in death;
When we heave the parting breath:
When our solemn doom is near,
Jesus, Son of Mary, hear!
Thou hast bowed the dying head;
Thou the blood of life hast shed;
Thou hast filled a mortal bier:
Jesus, Son of Mary, hear!

HYMN 1002.   7s & 5s or 7s.   J. E. S.

1. In the dark and cloud-y day, When earth's rich-es flee a - way,

And the last hope will not stay, Sav-iour, Sav-iour com-fort me!

2. When e se - cret i - dol's gone That my poor heart yearned up-on,—

Des - o - late, be - reft, a - lone, Sav-iour, Sav-iour, com-fort me!

3 Thou, who wast so sorely tried
In the darkness crucified,
Bid me in thy love confide;
Saviour, comfort me!

4 Comfort me; I am cast down:
'Tis my heavenly Father's frown;

I deserve it all, I own:
Saviour, comfort me!

5 So it shall be good for me
Much afflicted now to be,
If thou wilt but tenderly,
Saviour, comfort me!

HYMN 554.   7s & 6s.   J. E. S.

1. We stand in deep repentance, Before thy throne of love; O God of grace, for-
give us; The stain of guilt re - move; Be-hold us while with weep-ing We
lift our eyes to thee; And all our sins sub-du-ing, Our Father, set us free!

2 Oh! shouldst thou from us fallen
  Withold thy grace to guide,
For ever we should wander,
  From thee, and peace, aside;
But thou to spirits contrite
  Dost light and life impart,
That man may learn to serve thee
  With thankful, joyous heart.

3 Our souls— on thee we cast them,
  Our only refuge thou!
Thy cheering words revive us,
  When pressed with grief we bow:
Thou bear'st the trusting spirit
  Upon thy loving breast,
And givest all thy ransomed
  A sweet, unending rest.

HYMN 464. 7s & 6s.

J. E. S.

1. Droop-ing souls, no lon-ger mourn, Je-sus still is precious;

If to him you now re-turn, Heaven will be pro-pi-tious;

Je-sus now is pass-ing by, Call-ing wanderers near him;

Drooping souls, you need not die, Go to him and hear him!

2 He has pardons, full and free,
  Drooping souls to gladden;
Still he cries— "come unto me,
  Weary, heavy-laden!"
Though your sins like mountains high,
  Rise, and reach to heaven,
Soon as you on him rely,
  All shall be forgiven.

3 Precious is the Saviour's name,
  Dear to all that love him;
He to save the dying came;—
  Go to him and prove him!
Wandering sinners, now return;
  Contrite souls, believe him!
Jesus calls you, cease to mourn;
  Worship him; receive him.

WILLOW.

HYMN 1308.   7s & 6s. D.

J. E. S.

1. There is a land immor-tal, The beau-ti-ful of lands; Be-side its ancient por-tal A si-lent sen-try stands; He on-ly can un-do it, And open wide the door; And mortals who pass thro' it, Are mortals nev-er-more.

2 Though dark and drear the passage
That leadeth to the gate,
Yet grace comes with the message,
To souls that watch and wait;
And at the time appointed
A messenger comes down,
And leads the Lord's anointed
From cross to glory's crown.

3 Their sighs are lost in singing,
They're blessed in their tears;
Their journey heaven-ward winging,
They leave on earth their fears:
Death like an angel seemeth;
"We welcome thee," they cry;
Their face with glory beameth—
'Tis life for them to die!

PRAISE THE LORD.

HYMN 132. 7s & 6s D.

1. Praise the Lord who reigns a - bove, And keeps his courts below; Praise him for his

Unison.

boundless love, And all his greatness show! Praise him for his noble deeds; Praise him

for his matchless power; Him, from whom all good proceeds, Let earth and heaven adore.

2 Publish, spread to all around
　　The great Immanuel's name;
Let the gospel trumpet sound,
　　The Prince of peace proclaim!
Praise him, every tuneful string;
　　All the reach of heavenly art,
All the power of music bring,
　　The music of the heart.

3 Him, in whom they move and live,
　　Let every creature sing;
Glory to our Saviour give,
　　And homage to our King:
Hallowed be his name beneath,
　　As in heaven, on earth adored;
Praise the Lord in every breath,
　　Let all things praise the Lord.

HARTFORD.

HYMN 270. 8s & 7s. J. E. S.

1. God is love; his mer-cy brightens All the path in which we rove;
Bliss he wakes and woe he lightens; God is wis-dom, God is love.

2. Chance and change are bus-y ev-er; Man de-cays, and a-ges move;
But his mer-cy wa-neth never; God is wis-dom, God is love.

3 Ev'n the hour that darkest seemeth,
Will his changeless goodness prove;
From the gloom his brightness streameth,
God is wisdom God is love.

4 We with earthly cares entwineth
Hope and comfort from above:
Everywhere his glory shineth;
God is wisdom, God is love.

HYMN 1306. 8s & 7s. D.

1. Je - sus, blessed Me - di - a - tor! Thou the air - y path hast trod;

Thou the Judge, the Con-sum-ma-tor! Shepherd of the fold of God!

Can I trust a fel-low-be-ing? Can I trust an an-gel's care?

O thou mer-ci-ful All-see-ing! Beam a-round my spir-it there.

2 Blessed fold! no foe can enter;
  And no friend departeth thence;
Jesus is their sun, their centre,
  And their shield Omnipotence!
Blessed, for the Lamb shall feed them,
  All their tears shall wipe away,
To the living fountains lead them,
  Till fruition's perfect day.

3 Lo! it comes, that day of wonder!
  Louder chorals shake the skies:
Hades' gates are burst asunder;
  See! the new-clothed myriads rise!
Thought! repress thy weak endeavor;
  Here must reason prostrate fall;
Oh, the ineffable Forever!
  And the eternal All in All!

HARPER.

HYMN 265.   8s & 7s. D.   Arr.

1. Lord, thy glo - ry fills the hea - ven; Earth is
with its full - ness stored; Un - to thee be glo - ry
giv - en, Ho - ly, ho - ly, ho - ly Lord! Heaven is
still with an - thems ring-ing; Earth takes up the an - gels' cry,

Ho - ly, ho - ly, ho ly, sing - ing, Lord of

hosts, thou Lord most high, Lord of hosts, thou Lord most high.

2 Ever thus in God's high praises,
   Brethren, let our tongues unite,
While our thoughts his greatness raises,
   And our love his gifts excite:
With his seraph train before him,
   With his holy church below,
Thus unite we to adore him,
   Bid we thus our anthem flow.

3 Lord, thy glory fills the heavens;
   Earth is with its fullness stored;
Unto thee be glory given,
   Holy, holy, holy Lord!
Thus thy glorious name confessing,
   We adopt the angels' cry,
Holy, holy, holy, blessing
   Thee, the Lord our God most high!

WHILE WE LOWLY BOW.

HYMN 189.   8s, 7s & 4s.   Arr.

1. While we low - ly bow be - fore thee, Wilt thou, gracious Saviour, hear?

We are poor and need - y sinners, Full of doubt and full of fear;

Gracious Saviour, Gra - cious Saviour, Make us hum - ble and sin - cere.

2 Fill us with thy Holy Spirit;
  Sanctify us by thy grace;
Oh, incline us more to love thee,
  And in dust our souls abase,
    Hear us, Saviour,
  And unvail thy glorious face.

3 None in vain did ever ask thee
  For the Spirit of thy love;
Hear us, then, dear Saviour, hear us;
  Grant an answer from above;
    Blessed Saviour,
  Hear and answer from above.

OLIVE.

HYMN 1003.   8s & 6s.   Arr.

1. I ask not now for gold to gild, With mock-ing
shine, an ach - ing frame; The yearn-ing of the
mind is stilled— I ask not now for fame.

2 But, bowed in lowliness of mind,
  I make my humble wishes known;
  I only ask a will resigned,
  O Father, to thine own.

3 In vain I task my aching brain,
  In vain the sages' thoughts I scan;
  I only feel how weak I am,
  How poor and blind is man.

4 And now my spirit sighs for home,
  And longs for light whereby to see;
  And, like a weary child, would come,
  O Father, unto thee.

ABIDE WITH ME.

HYMN 785. 10s.

1. A - bide with me! Fast falls the e - ven - tide,

The dark - ness deep - ens— Lord, with me a - bide!

When oth - er help - ers fail, and com - forts flee,

Help of the help - less, oh, a - bide with me!

2. Swift to its close ebbs out life's lit - tle day,

Earth's joys grow dim, its glo - ries pass a - way;

Change and de - cay in all a - round I see;

O thou, who chang - est not, A - bide with me!

3 I need thy presence every passing hour,
What but thy grace can foil the tempter's power?
Who, like thyself my guide and stay can be?
Through cloud and sunshine, oh, abide with me!

4 Not a brief glance I long, a passing word,
But as thou dwell'st with thy disciples, Lord,
Familiar, condescending, patient, free,
Come, not to sojourn, but abide with me!

TALMA.

HYMN 688.   9s & 8s.   J. E. S.

1. Christian, the morn breaks sweet-ly o'er thee, And all the

mid - night shad - ows flee, Tinged are the dis - tant skies with

glo - ry, A bea - con light hung out for thee;

A - rise, a - rise! the light breaks o'er thee;

Thy name is gra - ven on the throne; Thy home is in the world of glo - ry, Where thy Re - deem - er reigns a - lone, Where thy Re - deem - er reigns a - lone.

2 Tossed on time's rude, relentless surges,
  Calmly composed, and dauntless stand,
For lo! beyond those scenes emerges
  The height that bounds the promised land:
Behold! behold! the land is nearing,
  Where the wild sea-storm's rage is o'er;
Hark! how the heavenly hosts are cheering,
  See in what throngs they range the shore!

3 Cheer up! cheer up! the day breaks o'er thee,
  Bright as the summer's noon-tide ray,
The star-gemmed crowns and realms of glory
  Invite thy happy soul away;
Away! away! leave all for glory,
  Thy name is graven on the throne;
Thy home is in that world of glory,
  Where thy Redeemer reigns alone.

PORTLAND.

HYMN 1225.   8s & 4s.   J. E. S.

1. There is a calm for those who weep, A rest for wea-ry pil-grims

found: They soft-ly lie, and sweet-ly sleep, Low in the ground.

2 The storm that racks the wintry sky
   No more disturbs their deep repose
Than summer evening's latest sigh,
   That shuts the rose.

3 I long to lay this painful head
   And aching heart beneath the soil;
To slumber in that dreamless bed,
   From all my toil.

4 The soul, of origin divine,
   God's glorious image, freed from clay,
In heaven's eternal sphere shall shine,
   A star of day.

5 The sun is but a spark of fire,
   A transient meteor in the sky:
The soul, immortal as its Sire,
   Shall never die.

1. Send kind - ly light a - mid th' en-cir - cling gloom, And lead me

on! The night is dark, and I am far from home;

Lead thou me on! Keep thou my feet; I do not ask to

see The dis - tant scene; one step's e - nough for me.

2. I was not ev-er thus, nor prayed that thou Should'st lead me
on! I lov'd to choose and see my path; but now
Lead thou me on! I lov'd day's daz-zling light, and
spite of fears, Pride ruled my will: re-member not past years!

3. So long thy pow'r hath blessed me, sure-ly still 'Twill lead me

on! Through drear-y doubt, through pain and sor-row, till

The night is gone, And with the morn those an-gel fa-ces smile Which

I have lov'd long since, and lost and lost a-while.

I ONCE WAS A STRANGER.

HYMN 924.   11s.

J. E. S.

1. I   once was a stranger   to   grace and to God;   I

knew not my dan-ger, and felt not my load; Tho' friends spoke in rapture of

Christ on the Tree, Je - ho - vah, my Saviour, seem'd nothing to me.

QUARTET.

Je - ho - vah, my Sav - iour, seem'd noth - ing to me.

2. When free grace a - woke me by light from on high, Then
3. My   ter - rors   all van - ished be - fore his sweet name; My
4. Je - ho - vah, the Lord, is   my treas - ure and boast; Je -
5. Ev'n tread-ing the val - ley, the shad - ow of death, This

le - gal fears shook me: I trembled to die: No re - fuge, no safe-ty, in
guilty fears banish'd, with boldness I came To drink at the fountain, so
hovah, my Saviour, I ne'er can be lost: In thee I shall conquer, by
watchword shall rally my fal - ter-ing breath; For, while from life's fe - ver my

self could I see: Je - ho - vah, thou on - ly my Saviour must be!
co - pious and free: Je - ho - vah, my Saviour, is all things to me.
flood and by field, Je - ho - vah my an - chor, Je - ho - vah my shield!
God sets me free, Je - ho - vah, my Saviour, my death-song shall be!

QUARTET.

Je - ho - vah, thou on - ly my Sav - iour must be!
Je - ho - vah, my Sav - iour, is all things to me.
Je - ho - vah my an - chor, Je - ho - vah my shield!
Je - ho - vah, my Sav - iour, my death-song shall be!

DALL.

J. E. S.

1. Be joy - ful in God, all ye lands of the earth;

Oh, serve him with glad - ness and fear; Ex - ult in his

pres - ence with mu - sic and mirth; With love and de -

vo - tion draw near. 2. For Jeho - vah is God, and Je -

ho - vah a - lone, Cre - a - tor and Rul - er o'er

all; And we are his peo - ple, his scep - tre we

own; His sheep, and we fol - low his call.

3 Oh, enter his gates with thanksgiving and song;
   Your vows in his temple proclaim;
   His praise with melodious accordance prolong,
   And bless his adorable name.

4 For good is the Lord, inexpressibly good,
   And we are the work of his hand;
   His mercy and truth from eternity stood,
   And shall to eternity stand.

EATON.

70

HYMN 141. 11s.   J. E. S.

1. Give glo-ry to God in the high-est; give praise, Ye no-ble, ye might-y, with joy-ful ac-cord; All-wise are his coun-sels, all-per-fect his ways; In the beauty of ho-li-ness worship the Lord.

2 At the voice of the Lord the strong cedars are bowed,
  And towers from their base into ruin are hurled;
The voice of the Lord, from the dark-bosomed cloud,
  Dissevers the lightning in flames o'er the world.

3 The voice of the Lord, through the calm of the wood,
  Awakens its echoes, strikes light through its caves;
The Lord sitteth King on the turbulent flood;
  The winds are his servants,—his servants the waves

4 The Lord is the strength of his people; the Lord
  Gives health to his chosen, and peace evermore;
Then throng to his temple, his glory record;
  But oh, when he speaketh,—in silence adore!

HYMN 627. P. M.

J. E. S.

1. Wilt thou not vis - it me? The plant be - side me feels thy gen - tle dew; Each blade of grass I see, From thy deep earth its quick - ening mois - ture drew.

2 Wilt thou not visit me?
  Thy morning calls on me with cheering tone;
And every hill and tree
  Lift but one voice, the voice of thee alone.

3 Come! for I need thy love,
  More than the flower the dew or grass the rain;
Come, like thy Holy Dove,
  And let me in thy sight rejoice to live again.

4 Yes! thou wilt visit me;
  Nor plant, nor trees, thine eye delights so well
As when from sin set free,
  Man's spirit comes with thine in peace to dwell.

PEACE.

HYMN 926. 6s & 4s.   Arr.

1. Peace, peace, I leave with you, My peace I give to you, Trust to my care!

My peace I give to you, Trust to my care!   Thus the Redeemer said,

And bowed his sacred head, Lone in the garden shade, Wrestling in prayer.

Lone in the gar - den shade, Wrestling in prayer. 2. Peace, peace, I
                                               3. Peace, peace, I

leave with you, My peace I give to you, Per - fect and pure;....
leave with you, My peace I give to you, Though foes in - vade;....

Per - fect and pure; Not as the world doth give, Words that the
Though foes in - vade; All power is given to me, I will your

soul deceive; Ye who in me be - lieve Shall rest se - cure.
ref - uge be, Now and e - ter - nal - ly, Be not dismayed!

D. S.

Ye who in me be - lieve, Shall rest se - cure.
Now and e - ter - nal - ly, Be not dis - mayed!

www.ingramcontent.com/pod-product-compliance
Lightning Source LLC
Chambersburg PA
CBHW020336090426
42735CB00009B/1561